"prod-*uh*kt spesh-*uh*-list"

How to be a *GOOD* one!

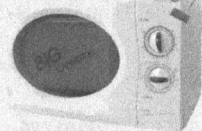

By **SIMMS THOMAS**
and **BOB THOMAS**

Southern Book Company
KNOXVILLE, TN

Published by the
Southern Book Company
Box 53112
Knoxville, Tennessee 37950
SouthernBookCo.com

www.ThePSBook.com

For more information on Simms Thomas go to SimmsThomas.com,
Bob Thomas, go to BTThomas.com

Comments and Letters:

Simms Thomas or Bob Thomas
C/O Southern Book Company
Box 53112
Knoxville, Tennessee 37950

Email: Simms@SimmsThomas.com, BT@BTThomas.com

ISBN: 978-0-9801876-1-8

Book Cover and Interior Design by Daniel Middleton
www.scribefreelance.com

Printed in the United States of America

THE PRODUCT SPECIALIST HANDBOOK

———

How to be a good Product Specialist . . . and by the way,
what *IS* a Product Specialist?

The purpose of this book is to educate and empower those who are entrusted with the task of not only representing a product, but with disseminating information about that product. When a product's benefits are fully understood, the public is then able to make better decisions about which products to purchase.

It is our hope that every Product Specialist will be able to improve their communication skills, master the art of representing themselves and their respective products, learn to use their time wisely, and become more knowledgeable in the process of understanding and identifying potential customers when meeting consumers.

To our dads, Walt and Wally. They were two of the best "people persons" anyone ever met.

TABLE OF CONTENTS

" Each year the average household spends over $28K on items other than housing or food. "

— US Dept. of Labor Statistics

Chapter One
THE BASIC QUESTIONS

- What is a Product Specialist?

> **Specialist:** *Someone who devotes themselves to some specialty; works collaboratively with others and is dedicated to a specific product or skill.*
>
> **Product:** *A commodity offered for sale or offered as something that is produced by human or mechanical effort or by a natural process.*

Given the above definitions, a *PRODUCT SPECIALIST,* (or PS) *must* be someone who devotes themselves to a product that is offered for sale. But it is not a true statement to say that a Product Specialist is one who simply specializes in a product, because a PS is far more. A Product Specialist isn't easy to define. A PS becomes the face and voice of a product. A Product Specialist influences consumers, works closely with sales personnel, provides feedback from consumers, and relays information to consumers regarding a product — *IF* they are doing their job right. But, before you get to the front line, you have to know your product, and you have to know to whom you are trying to sell your product.

Before we get started, let's go over a simple checklist that a Product Specialist should follow.

CHECKLIST

- You must continue to educate yourself on the product
- You need to understand the client's goals
- You need a great work ethic
- You must be punctual
- You should maintain good personal grooming and hygiene habits
- You must have respect for yourself and others
- You should find pleasure in your work

It all sounds fairly simple, right? So why is it that so many people find these tasks so hard to grasp? The following pages address this and other interesting questions that will enable you to better understand the role of a Product Specialist.

HOW CAN A PRODUCT SPECIALIST HELP THE CONSUMER?

> **Consumer:** *A person who uses goods or services.*

One of the most important aspects of a Product Specialist's job is to help consumers become as knowledgeable as possible about a product on which they are planning to spend their hard earned money. To facilitate this, a PS must inform consumers about which products best meet their needs. When consumers make purchases that satisfy their desires and needs, the market is better served and supply and demand will function more efficiently. Demand would force increased production and bring about a higher quality of products that would enable all of us to live our lives with less stress, and hopefully with more pleasure.

PRODUCT KNOWLEDGE

- What is the History of Your Product?

Many potential customers may want to know the historical facts about your product. Who thought of the concept? Who invented it? How did it originate? How has it evolved over time? The answers to these questions are important because they provide the consumer with background information about your product and allows them to get a feel as to where your product and possibly their purchase — is going to be in years to come.

Oftentimes the history of a product opens up avenues of discussion with potential customers and addresses many of their concerns, among which is the question of whether your product will continue to be viable in the future. A Product Specialist should make an effort to know not only the history of their product, but also the current leadership positions and owners of the company. Generally, people like to be in the know and want to feel good about their purchase, whether it is one of necessity or pleasure or both. The more informed the consumer is as a direct result of the efforts of you, the Product Specialist, the more comfortable they will feel spending their money on your product.

- How Does Your Product Work?

A Product Specialist should have a full understanding of how the product they are representing operates. They should be able to explain its exact function or usefulness in detail to prospective buyers, and in order to accomplish this they need to actually use the product if possible. Obviously, if the product is gender specific, or designed for use by experts, such as medical equipment, etc., you aren't going to have the opportunity to "try it out." But beyond that, nothing quite equates with the real life experience of using the product, because it enables the PS to have a personal evaluation of the product and lends more credibility to their product knowledge. Through personal use you may discover a more in-depth degree of understanding of your product, and that information may be useful during conversations with consumers.

By drawing upon your real life experience with a product, this will keep you from falling into the repeat pattern trap as well. Sometimes it is easier to just relay what you have been told from a trainer or facilitator. But you need to challenge yourself and take your knowledge a step farther. The combination of mixing facts you have learned with the experience of real life product use becomes a powerful conversation tool. Not only does this provide people with an example of how your product can be used, but it will also become more sincere and believable when the public hears and understands how you, the Product Specialist, have used the product and how they might use it as well.

- What Are the Advantages of Your Product?

A good Product Specialist will know what their product brings to the marketplace that other similar products do not. Additionally, developers or manufacturers usually make something because they have discovered a better way to do so, or have improved on an idea to produce a product that does something that others do not. A seasoned Product Specialist will be intimately familiar with that product's advantage. Very rarely does a new product do the same thing as a similar product which already exists, *UNLESS* they have found a way to make the same product for less — thus saving the consumer money — or found a way to make it better. Both are advantages for the consumer. Find the advantages of your product so you can better educate the buying public.

- Should A Product Specialist Like (or believe in) the Product?

The best approach a Product Specialist can take is to understand the positive attributes of the product along with the beneficial qualities it possesses so they are prepared to convey these benefits and attributes to the consumer. It is important to note that every product has shortcomings. Nothing is flawless, and consumers will have various opinions regarding what they expect from the product.

- Can You Identify the Competition?

There are some people who believe you should know your

competitor's products as well as your own. While it is important to be aware of, informed about, and to understand the highlights of your competitor's product, to labor over it until you know it as well as your own is an unreasonable expectation. Since the marketplace and products are constantly evolving, it is difficult to "know it all." If you know your product well, and continue to educate and update your knowledge of your product, then you will be able to assist consumers who ask significant questions as they relate to your competition.

- How will you know what the Public's Perception of your Product is, and is this important?

A Product Specialist will know fairly quickly whether or not the public likes or dislikes their product. To obtain the public's opinion all you have to do is listen. But, you actually should go deeper than just listening to others' opinions of your product. Keep up to date by reading trade magazines; actively scan newspapers for topics that relate to your product; "Google" your product; read blogs about it; and, ultimately, when the situation presents itself, ask people you meet outside of the product display arena about your product. It is important to know how your product is perceived. The more information you have the better you are able to either combat a negative or false opinion about your product.

66 *75% of people don't believe that companies tell the truth in advertisements.* **99**

—Yankelovich

Chapter Two
MEETING THE PUBLIC

> **Public:** *Populace: people in general considered as a whole; not private; open to or concerning the people as a whole; a body of people sharing some common interest.*

A *Product Specialist will meet* the public by the hundreds and in some situations by the thousands in a single day. So knowing how to best serve the consumer and still attain your goal of telling your product's story is essential. A PS needs to efficiently and effectively convey the many benefits of the product to the greatest number of people in a given amount of time. But, how is that possible? There are four steps that are helpful: Connecting, Engaging, Being Efficient, and finally, the Closure.

CONNECTING WITH THE PUBLIC

> **Connecting:** *The process of bringing ideas or events together*

Sometimes when you meet someone for the first time, you feel as if a connection has been made. That is what you are striving for when meeting the public. You need to make a connection, whether that means approaching them and making eye contact, or simply being in a position to engage in verbal communication with them, that initial connection will lay the foundation for any future rapport. Therefore, if your stage is a display floor in a store, a convention center, an auto show, a mall, or any place where products are demonstrated, the PS must make him or herself available to the consumer for the connection to take place.

- Keeping your arms open and not folded is an invitation into your space. Some may not know that when you cross your arms and fold them across your chest you are sending out the message: "Stay away from me, I am busy."
- Keep your hands out of your pockets, not in your pockets. This prevents you from sending the message that you are bored.
- Keep your toes pointed toward the person to whom you are talking, otherwise you will send the message that you are thinking of exiting.
- Don't position your fingers in a steeple style as this may send a message that you believe you are in power.
- Keep a smile on your face. Yes, smile. Smiling is very important. When a person smiles, the pitch of their voice changes, and to the human ear a smile helps create a more pleasant and inviting sound. Try it sometime.
- Keep your eyes open. Of course you are not going to keep your eyes closed. What we mean is make eye contact with as

any people as possible without staring.

People will respond to those who look at them with a pleasant smile, friendly body language, and a sincere greeting. Even a simple "hello" can lead to a connection when someone enters your exhibit space. So you smile, greet the consumer, and make a connection. Now you need to keep the connection strong and keep it going.

1. Introduce your product to the consumer by telling them it exists
2. Convey to the consumer the many benefits of your product
3. Find the association between the consumer and your product
4. Summarize how your product's benefits will benefit the consumer

Connecting with the consumer is all about successfully delivering the message to the masses that your product needs their attention and that they should devote their attention to your information.

ENGAGE YOUR AUDIENCE

Engage: *To carry out or participate in an activity; be involved in.*

After a connection has been established you must then engage the consumer. For example, if your product is a vehicle, you may want to offer correct product information, such as: "This vehicle was the SUV of the Year." You should supply the consumer with information loaded with various generic talking points that concerns your product. When you engage the consumer several things can take place:

1. The customer responds positively, i.e., "It was?" "What made it so special?" From this point it is important to move on to the relationship building level. Just a few minutes of informed conversation can lead to the start of a relationship that can develop and ultimately result in a sale.

2. The customer does not respond with positive feedback, but their body language suggests they are possibly interested in your product. This is an excellent opportunity for the PS to provide additional dialogue. The goal is to provide the consumer with as much information as possible regarding the product by highlighting how it can benefit them and their needs. This particular approach will strengthen and continue to build the relationship.

3. The customer may ignore you. If this is the case, a PS needs to realize that they are there to inform and engage, not to irritate and bother. This would be the time to step away from the spotlight and release the customer.

Be Efficient With Your Time

> *Efficient:* Being effective without wasting time or effort or expense.

It is quite easy to get caught up in a conversation with someone visiting your display area. However, Product Specialists should be aware of a consumer's reason for looking at a product. A PS needs to be able to differentiate between a potential customer and someone who literally just stopped by to chat. And that can be quite difficult.

1. Are they are talker? A talker will make one believe they are a fabulous PS, soaking up every point you discuss, asking questions regarding the benefits of a product and would generally be willing to spend hours with you. This is when a PS needs to develop the skill of knowing the difference of information being transferred to interested parties and information being transferred to someone who is "shooting the breeze" as the saying goes. By recognizing the appropriate amount of time, energy, and effort being put forth, a PS can learn to redirect the talker. Otherwise, a PS may discover their precious time has been taken by the talker when it could have been better spent with a potential customer.

2. Are they truly a potential customer? A customer will also ask questions and (hopefully) think you are a fabulous PS, but primarily they want information they don't already have. A talker will generally have some information and won't keep on task, which means discussing just the product, but will tend to discuss everyday matters of the world with you as well. A potential customer is visiting you for a reason. They want and need information about your product and you are the person who can give them what they need. Be careful not to get bogged down with the talker when you need to be with the potential consumer.

3. If necessary, put time limits on your conversations with consumers. Over the course of time, you will develop an accurate sense of who is truly interested in your product and who is just "shooting the breeze." By being efficient with your time, you will be better able to serve and assist more people. You will also be able to be more fluid at identifying who you are talking to and make the assessment of either to release the talker, continue to provide valuable information, or finally to refer someone in the direction of a salesperson to perhaps get the consumer closer to becoming a true customer. By sending them in the direction of a sales associate through your engagement, the sales goal is closer to becoming a reality.

CLOSURE

> **Closure:** *Approaching a particular destination; a coming closer; a narrowing of a gap.*

Closure doesn't necessarily mean securing or finalizing a deal. Sure, that's the ultimate goal. It would be a huge bonus if everyone who visited your exhibit space bought your product. But, that isn't going to happen. What should happen is that you professionally present and deliver information to the public. Closure should be in the form of a satisfied potential customer who has walked into your display area, has talked with you, the PS, and has left with viable information in hand, including the benefits of your product, how the purchase of your product would affect them, and how and where to obtain your product. Hopefully, with the information you have provided, a sale will be forthcoming.

In summary, remember the rules of **CONNECT**, **ENGAGE**, being **EFFICIENT WITH TIME**, and **CLOSEURE**.

- Open yourself up physically to welcome visitors and potential customers
- Avoid spending too much quality time with an individual when a salesperson is present to facilitate a deal

- Don't become so involved with how great you are doing while building a relationship (becoming a talker yourself) that you lose sight of the goal to educate
- Move people through the pipeline — meet them, inform them, lead them to a salesperson if necessary

Your job is not to see how many people you can talk to, but how many people you can make aware of your product by informing them of its benefits in an efficient and timely manner, so that they will want to become a future buyer of your product.

YOU CAN'T PLEASE EVERYONE

In the job description of Product Specialist, making every person you meet on the show floor happy is not on the list. No matter how hard you try, it's just not possible. You will come into contact with people who have preconceived ideas and opinions regarding your product. These ideas and opinions may be negative, and there isn't much you can say that will change their beliefs, be they valid or not. Perhaps they have used your product and weren't satisfied. Perhaps a friend or family member had a bad experience. There are a few helpful things you should do when placed in these situations:

- Listen to their issues
- Provide them with the best product information and support possible
- Direct them to other avenues for voicing complaints

- Take complaints seriously, not personally

Sometimes people just want someone to listen to their complaints. They want someone to empathize with them. All products, as we stated, will have flaws — no exceptions — even if the flaws fall into the "It doesn't fit my lifestyle" category or "It doesn't come in the color I want." But oftentimes, consumer feedback (complaints included) if properly channeled, can lead to positive changes in a product. Continual upgrading, the implementation of better designs, and additional uses or functions are among the favorable improvements products achieve when consumer complaints and general feedback are taken seriously.

You will also encounter those who, while they may still like and use your product, have a legitimate complaint and need assistance on a level that you cannot provide. This is when you can direct them to a company website, telephone number, a particular individual, or address to which they can correspond. All of these suggestions are essential, because you are providing helpful information, and you are taking their complaint seriously, but not personally, because it is not about *you*.

The client or manufacturer should provide instructions to assist you in handling consumer complaints. They should provide you with all the necessary information so that the consumer can leave the show floor feeling as if they were allowed to voice their concerns and complaints and have additional information in hand should they decide to take further action with someone within the company other than you if needed.

Of course, you may also encounter those individuals who have no intention of purchasing your product. They are there to criticize. You need to recognize those individuals and treat them with the same courtesy as all others. Remember, your role is to inform the public about your product to the best of your ability. As long as you do that, you are doing your job.

HOW TO MAKE AN IMPRESSION ON AN UNSUSPECTING PUBLIC

> **Unsuspecting**: *Not knowing or being aware of.*

You, the PS, are the front line for your company. The role of a PS is unlike that of a salesperson, because a salesperson will generally have an initial encounter with a consumer who may be a potential customer when the consumer has made the first effort by stepping into a place of business. As a Product Specialist, you will often meet people who have no intention of making a commitment to your product. They may be unaware of or know nothing about your product. That's where you come in with your valuable knowledge and information. But, in order for them to be most receptive to that information, you need to make a good impression. It is your job to impress people when they are not expecting to be impressed.

> *Impression:* An outward appearance or vague idea in which some confidence is placed.

Have you ever had a lasting memory from some insignificant occurrence or event in your life that seems like it took place yesterday? Not a marriage or other monumental occurrence, but maybe an encounter with someone who showed, explained, or demonstrated something to you in such an interesting way that, over the years, you have never forgotten it. That's not going to be everyone's experience when they talk to you, but it isn't a bad goal to strive for. Every time you have the opportunity to discuss your product with the public, think outside the box and get creative as you relate how your product meets their needs. Strive for the "ah ha" reaction when you explain how your product works so that they will readily grasp the unique and/or unexpected things your product can do. That kind of impression — the kind that the customer is still thinking about as they walk away or will recall when your product, or similar products, are considered for purchase — is what you want to cultivate.

> *Charisma:* A personal attractiveness or interestingness that enables you to influence others.

If you are trying to impress someone, a little bit of charisma can go a long way. Regardless of what you read in celebrity magazines, charisma is not an innate trait. It is a skill someone hones and cultivates over time when working with the public. It starts with:

- Sincerely listening to people
- Looking them in the eyes
- Understanding their needs
- Gaining their attention and keeping it

After these steps have successfully been mastered, a charismatic person will then proceed to lay the foundation of the history or story of the product. This person has the ability to transform the showroom into their stage as they share the important aspects of their product in relation to the consumer's needs. People can change their opinions on a dime from bad (or indifferent) to good if they believe in you. In the same way, someone who is not impressed by you can change their opinion from good to bad just as quickly.

"It takes the average consumer 21.41 seconds to decide which toaster to buy."

—G.R. Foxall, Consumer behavior Analysis

Chapter Three

CATEGORIZING THE CONSUMER—WHAT IS IT?

Want more insight into identifying real customers? Well, as you know, the public is an unknown entity. When working as a PS the people you encounter may be employees of the venue, people spending time with friends or family, your competition, your factory representatives, *OR* they may be potential customers. It is your job as the Product Specialist to know who is who.

Categorizing, or simply sizing people up can help you do your job better. People look at categorizing in different ways. But first, this is not an invitation to eliminate anyone; instead, you are to decide where people are on the potential purchasing scale. A PS needs to know how to best serve the public by devoting the correct amount of time and energy to those who are more serious about buying their product. The process is not foolproof; there will be exceptions, and you should always be ready for the exceptions and be able to identify them as quickly as possible. There will always be a few who will look, act, dress, and talk as if they would never be a potential customer when, in reality, they buy everything your company has to sell. Always remember that regardless whether you think a person is a potential buyer or not, you should always treat each person with respect and kindness. Our goal here is to help you best decide who to spend more time with than others.

With that said, as you represent a product over a period of time, you should be able to determine in about one minute which one of the following four "P" categories the person standing in front of you belongs to.

1. **THE PASSERBY** — As the title suggests, this person can literally be just passing by your display area with no interest in buying. However, to entertain themselves, they will ask questions, take samples, watch demonstrations — as long as their time allows — and then leave, never to be seen again. Once more, always treat these people and others with respect, as they may surprise you and take the next step. But unless they do, don't spend too much time with them if you have other customers present. In this case, if there are others present that you could talk to, greet the Passerby warmly, offer them a brochure, and give them the opportunity to go to the next level with you. If they don't respond accordingly, then wish them a wonderful day with an open invitation to return at anytime.

2. **THE POSSIBLE** — The Possible will do more than the Passerby. He or she will know about your product and may have a probing question or two. But, more than likely, they will not be overly inquisitive. When asked whether they own your product or one of its competitors, their response will be short. The Possible could become a customer, but it will take many visits to bring them to the point of purchase. Therefore, give them all the courtesies that the Passerby was afforded, and explain or demonstrate

how your product can benefit them and how they can justify buying your product.

3. **THE POTENTIAL** — The Potential will know your product more than the average interested consumer. They may already own a previous version or model of your product or a competitor's comparable product. This type needs to be updated and reassured on key points that will reinforce their decision to purchase your product for the first time or as a repeat buyer. Chances are the Potential is already considering a purchase and will be requesting more detailed information about pricing, servicing, new equipment and benefits, and the steps involved in becoming a purchaser. A Product Specialist needs to recognize the Potential so they can take them to the next level and facilitate a sale.

4. **THE PURCHASER** — The Purchaser is ready to do just that, make a purchase. They know the product, have researched the product, and have either talked to you or someone like you several times. At this point, the Purchaser needs only to find a specific version of your product that best suits their needs and possibly obtain price points that work within their budget.

WHY DO YOU CATEGORIZE?

It's important to at least have a general idea and guideline to follow so that you can better serve the consumers you meet. By keeping the above four categories in mind when you meet the general public you will be better able to distinguish between:

- Those strolling through to peruse the inventory
- Those who need additional attention
- Those seeking individual answers to more in-depth questions
- Those who are armed with knowledge and only need specific information to close the deal

" It takes the average woman 21.01 seconds to decide which dress to buy. "

—G.R. Foxall, Consumer behavior Analysis

Chapter Four

LET'S GET PERSONAL:
CHARACTERISTICS OF A GOOD SPECIALIST

> **Pride**: *A feeling of self-respect and personal worth; satisfaction with your achievements.*

Pride *takes on many forms*. Some people live by it; some wear it on their sleeve while others could not care less about it. We all need a healthy dose of pride. Pride is that part of you that says, "Well done," at the end of the day. When you have pride in your work, you do your job to the best of your ability in the manner in which you were instructed. If pride is absent, or if someone feels their job is beneath them, they will do as little as necessary believing it doesn't make a difference. They may even think, "This isn't my real job so why bother." This is wrong.

Failing to do the job you have agreed to do can harm you in two ways. It can weaken your character and it can damage your reputation. And these are two assets you need to succeed as a Product Specialist.

> **Character**: *Attribute that determines a person's moral and ethical actions and reactions.*

For a while, you may be able to fool your employer, your family, and your friends, but your character is always watching. Think of it like this: every person is born with a flawless shield of character. What we do with our character as we live our lives either strengthens or weakens that shield. At the end of the day you can't hide your character, because it is always evaluating you and giving you a report. The more you allow your character to be weakened, the less you have to offer. As a Product Specialist, you need to keep your shield strong, because your character can be considered a reflection of the product's character.

> **Reputation**: *The general estimation that the public has for a person; the opinion of the public toward a person, a group, or an organization.*

Guess what? Everyone is watching you. They watch how you respond to adversity and success, how you treat others, and how you do your job. We are judged by others, and that judgment is formed from observation; they form an opinion as to whether they want to be like you or nothing like you. They assess how you respond in any given situation and regard the quality of the work you perform. They are grading you in a sense, either by word of mouth, through evaluations, or during direct interactions with you.

Some may say they don't care what others think about them. If the "others" are of high character, then they should care, because they are the very ones who will either buy your product or pass positive or negative comments along to others about your product. Companies spend millions of dollars trying to cultivate a good reputation. It is quite important for the Product Specialist to put forth the best effort possible in maintaining that reputation.

When we give others proof that we have very little pride in our work, we chip away at our character and our reputation. Good or bad, your character and your reputation count and are hovering over you right now. You are the one who made them what they are today. If you don't think either of yours is of the highest quality, then change them. With determination, persistence, dependability, honesty, and a lot of hard work, they can be rebuilt. It is a powerful and rewarding experience to walk into a room filled with people and realize that your good reputation and solid character have preceded you. It is hard not to be a valued Product Specialist when you carry a good reputation with pride along with a solid character.

A LIST OF DOS AND DON'TS . . . OR WHAT IS REALLY IMPORTANT

The DOs:

DO HAVE A GOOD ATTITUDE

- Leave your personal problems at home

Your co-workers and clients deserve you — without any baggage.

- Decide to feel good

No one feels great all of the time. But you need to bring the best version of 100%-prepared, willing-worker-available to the floor every day.

- Be positive, hopeful, and expectant

Bring these attributes to work with you every day to help you succeed.

- Be a Scout

The Scout Law has some excellent words to work by: trustworthy, helpful, friendly, courteous, and cheerful . . . not a bad way to start *EVERY* day.

DO MAKE A STYLE EFFORT

We assume we don't need to talk about personal hygiene, such as showering or bathing. We do, however, need to address the importance of having a neat, finished, and polished appearance.

- The extra step counts

Those who take their physical appearance a step beyond the basics will often illicit comments such as "I don't know what it is I like about that person, but I like them." They project something extra. These are the people who don't just take a quick glance in the mirror; they make sure both their front and back look great. They are always stylish, whether that means a fresh haircut, or hair that is spiked, curled, gelled, or sprayed. Whatever suits them best, it's done. Even a person with a "punk" look representing a skateboard line can make sure their disorganized hair is perfect.

- The effort effect

People will notice when you put forth the effort to look your best — not just every once in a while but every day. Remember, today could be the day when the most important person — be it a client, customer, management official, or potential employer — walks through the door and meets you for the first time. Will you be ready? Those moments change lives. If you are single, you never know when your potential future spouse is going to walk up and say hello. This all goes back to the old Scout Motto: Be Prepared!

DO KNOW WHEN YOU ARE "ON"

- When do I start work?

When you are a Product Specialist, you have to know when you are "on" and when you are "off". Some might argue that a PS is always ON and that may be true to some extent. There are definite clear points in time which are important. You are "on" at these times:

1. The moment you walk on the show floor and the consumer has the opportunity to meet you
2. All the rest of the time

Like it or not, you are associated with your product. If you travel for your company, from the moment you arrive in a city to work, until the moment you leave, you will come in contact with many people outside of the showroom arena. To many of these people you are seen as the person from the XYZ Company. They associate you with the company by either talking to you and your co-workers directly, by handling your billing information, i.e. hotels, or something as simple as seeing your name tag as you go to and from work. These individuals will form opinions about your company, and subsequently, your product, based on their interactions with, and observations of, you. People form opinions and assign an unseen value to the product you represent based on their opinion of you, the PS. If you have presented an image of an impressive, trusted individual, that impressive, trusted feeling will be passed on to your product as an extra value. After all, how could someone as impressive as you represent an inferior product? However, the same can apply if someone has a negative impression of you. They will pass the negative image onto your product. No one wants to buy a product from someone they dislike or deem irresponsible.

Hey, that sounds like pride, character, and reputation all coming together to impress upon people the quality of your product. They DO make a difference and DO matter!

DO FOLLOW WARDROBE RULES

The wardrobe you wear while representing a product is usually selected by various people ranging from a stylist, wardrobe manager, client, or corporate leaders. Wardrobe decisions may be as simple as personal choice of style or color, or through exhaustive research coupled with favorable feedback from consumers. The choices may be a combination of both.

The point is this: time and thought, research, availability, and creative input — in other words an entire process — has taken place. A lot of energy and money has been spent selecting a uniform or wardrobe for the Product Specialist to wear.

The wardrobe could consist of tailored suits and shirts all color coordinated to be worn on certain days at particular events. The wardrobe may even consist of your own clothes, with the sole wardrobe directive being that you "wear khakis and a nice shirt." If this is the case, it is wise to put some effort into your selection, especially if you are going to be reimbursed. If you are spending your own money and have been given a description, no matter how basic, buy the best you can afford. There are numerous retailers that provide quality clothing and selections at value prices. Purchase clothes that fit you well today, look up to date, wear well, match, and are comfortable. Don't buy clothes with the idea that

"They will fit great when I lose five pounds," or "It doesn't fit, but it was on sale."

Depending on the product, the client, the avenue of sales of the product, and, of course, the budget, your wardrobe may be designer clothing and expensive. If you are accustomed to wearing these brands, then you will know how to care for them. But a lot of people starting out in business don't have the funds for costly clothing purchases. When a PS is instructed to have their wardrobe dry cleaned, this does not mean to wash the clothes on delicate. Until the wardrobe becomes yours personally, (if it ever becomes your own) treat it as though it is borrowed. Is it worth your job to transform a perfect fitting size 6 to a size 2? Take care of all clothing pieces as if they were your own, wear them as intended, and don't change or embellish any item.

DO KEEP LEARNING ABOUT YOUR PRODUCT

Things change fast in our world. Technology that was lightning fast last year is now slow. This means your knowledge base must not only keep up with the ever changing world, but also the advances of your product and the environment in which your product must now compete. There is no excuse for maintaining an average amount of product knowledge regarding your product, or above average product knowledge for that matter. You simply cannot possess the "I know enough" attitude. Knowing enough may get you by in today's market for a while. But just be aware — there is always someone smarter, more eager, more appreciative, more grateful, and more willing to do your job that will KNOW more and LEARN more about your product.

AND NOW, THE LIST OF THE DON'TS:

DON'T BECOME COMPLACENT

> **Complacent:** *Pleased with oneself or merits; contented to a fault with oneself or one's action.*

Taking your job for granted, or believing that you do your job so well that there is no room for improvement could be a major ingredient for failure. One needs to make a concerted effort each and every day to not only appreciate what one does have, but to study the product, reintroduce oneself and one's approach to the product. Do not fall victim to the thought process that you know it all. No matter how well you actually do know your product, there's always something else to learn. It is a continuing education process.

DON'T GET STUCK IN THE COMFORT ZONE

> **Comfort Zone:** *A behavioral state in which a person operates in an anxiety neutral condition, using a limited set of behaviors to deliver a steady level of performance, usually without a sense of risk.*

That definition says so much. It says GET OUT OF YOUR COMFORT ZONE. Highly successful people usually have to step out of their own comfort zone in order to accomplish a higher level of success, new and different responses, and expose themselves to different mental conditions and acceptance. *IF* they continually lean on and rely on their entire "comfortable" repertoire of information, then they cannot truly optimize or enhance their skills. So, every now and then, step out of your comfort zone and open yourself up to some new approach.

DON'T BECOME A SLACKER

Slacker: A person who shirks his work or duty; procrastinates, lacking a sense of direction in life and is an underachiever.

I don't know about you, but I don't want this person on my team. The best way to avoid being a slacker is to be a self starter, a go-getter, and to be proactive. You should start your job over every day. Make use of every day's opportunity.

DON'T BE AN AVOIDER

Avoider: avoids, shuns, escapes.

It is kind of hard to be a Product Specialist if you are an avoider. But, some avoiders do make it into the pack. This person will avoid contact with the public, which is rather ironic, since dealing with the public is their job. They may find menial tasks to perform on a constant basis in order to look busy. This may range from getting coffee, or running errands, to stocking unnecessary literature. However, an avoider can be helped. They should either find another job or attach themselves to someone who they feel can help them or empower them to complete the company's mission. Hopefully, they will have the opportunity to become armed with the needed knowledge and abilities to turn off their avoidance and start engaging the public. If not, then no one ever said this job was for everyone.

DON'T BE AN ARROGANT AVENGER

Arrogant: *Excessive pride in oneself; superior manner toward others, unwarranted importance.*
Avenger: *takes vengeance.*

Surprisingly enough, there are a few arrogant avengers among us, simply because they do know their product well they possess an attitude about their knowledge. They become overly impressed with their own knowledge and adapt a persona that can easily be passed to the consumer. This type of Product Specialist has become so knowledgeable that they are insulted when the public keeps asking "stupid" questions. What they fail to realize is that John or Suzy Q. Public doesn't know the answer to the questions they have just asked (that is why they are asking) nor are they privy to the fact that the last ten people you encountered may have asked the same question. It is important for a Product Specialist to remember two things:

1. Realize the repeated questions must be important, and the company needs to know what they pertain to
2. Become an ambassador, not a avenger

It is important to note here that companies should find out what the top five consumer inquiries are with regard to their products. It is the easiest way to discover any shortcomings their public relations message or their product in general may have. Any company that knows the top questions being asked repeatedly yet does nothing, is only wasting the valuable talents of their Product Specialists.

DON'T JUST LOOK AHEAD

> **Means to an end**: *refers to any action of which the sole purpose is to achieve something else.*

The Product Specialist who is working the job as a "means to an end" may be working at a very low level of commitment, contribution, and participation. In this day and age, few people have jobs they consider their final jobs (unless we're talking specialized professionals, such as doctors, lawyers, etc., but even they continue the learning process). Today, careers and lifestyles change more frequently than they have in the past. Having a job that is "a means to an end" is not a bad thing. But, to be short-sighted and not doing your job with the maximum amount of effort is wrong.

The mindset has to do with one's work ethic. If you agree to do a job, then you owe it, yes "owe it" to that employer to do that particular job to the very best of your ability. You aren't doing the employer a favor by agreeing to take their job offer, given training, trust, and skills and then not perform to the best of your ability. One should never take a job they do not intend on doing well.

Although some of us may have encountered someone who has taken a job and then dismisses the rules of ethics and does as little as possible to get by (the slacker, the avoider), bear in mind that, at some point, the rest of the team will notice and yes, eventually the client will as well. Remember, sometimes one's greatest opportunity comes about because someone else observed them doing a job to the best of their ability, and that trait is in great demand.

" Each year the average household spends more on transportation than they do on food. "

—US Dept of Labor Statistics

Chapter Five
HOW TO SUCCEED AS A TEAM

In *the last section*, we mentioned the word team. Usually when you work as a Product Specialist, you will work with other Product Specialists. But, instead of being a group of individuals, you need to be a team.

A team can do more than a group of individuals. Anyone can gather or combine a variety of individuals, assign them to work toward a common goal, and label them a team. But this really doesn't constitute a team because that is not the true spirit of the definition.

> ***Team***: *A group of individuals, usually from multiple disciplines, that drives and participates in the improvement process; cohesive group all striving to promote an issue or case forward for the good of all.*

DOES THIS SOUND LIKE *YOUR* TEAM?

- Everyone's focused on promoting the product
- Collectively, the team has great knowledge
- Each individual seeks self improvement to strengthen the overall team

No matter the arena, teams are made up of people with different strengths and weaknesses. People are hired for their strengths, which will fill the holes in the performance of the team where weaknesses exist. Championship sports teams never win on the strength of one; it takes a combined effort of everyone doing what they do best to enable the team to succeed.

> *Teamwork: Cooperative or coordinated effort on the part of a group of persons acting together as a team or in the interests of a common cause, unison for a higher cause, people working together for a selfless purpose, and so on.*

EMBRACE THE DIFFERENCES

Since the individuals on a team will encompass a myriad of different backgrounds, education, and life experiences, it is beneficial to recognize each other's weaknesses and/or lack of experiences or vastness of experience. This is to further promote a particular product and thereby reach a customer. If a PS knows he or she is not the best person to reach a particular customer or if they feel they do not have the expertise in an area, then the PS needs to be able to identify another team member who might be more suitable to talk with that consumer. It is called teamwork.

CONFLICTS

> **Conflict**: *An open clash between two opposing groups or individuals; a state of opposition between persons/ideas or interests.*

So, if you have a combination of all types of people from various backgrounds, with varying degrees of knowledge, and various academic achievements, etc., it might go without saying that there will be conflicts within the ranks. Each person will bring something different to the table, so to speak. Different levels of motivation. Different levels of dedication to the job. Different combinations of their own physical and emotional capacities. Not everyone is going to be compatible with one another.

HOW TO HANDLE CONFLICTS

First, don't take it personally. It's business. One factor that holds a lot of people back from real success is the ability to resolve differences.

> **Resolution**: *finding a solution to a problem; an agreement or outcome of decision making.*

This is where a supervisor/manager comes into play. Each team or organization needs a clear and precise path so that their plans and goals can be fully understood and implemented. A clear channel of communication must be established so that a priority of order can take place and tasks can be performed adequately. This person must have the ability to allow the convergence of many diverse opinions and allow creative ideals and ideas to come together. An effective coordinator assists the team in reaching their goals. Conflicts can run the gamut from trivial to basic to serious. Instead of pointing the finger at who is not doing something correctly, a supervisor or manager needs to point to resolutions, recognizing individual achievements and performances, and guiding each contribution in a direction that enables the group to come together and unite as they contribute to the common goal.

> **Leadership:** *Those entities that perform one or more acts of leading. The ability to affect human behavior so as to guide or inspire others.*

The concept of leadership is a process by which a person influences others to accomplish an objective, a goal, or a task, and directs the group in a way that makes it more cohesive, coherent, and obtainable. To lead others in attaining a goal — or more importantly to have others follow — is much different than just bossing people around. *ANYONE* can be a boss, but a leader possesses candor, skill, character, ethics, values, knowledge, and selfless service for the product, with a clear sense of direction, honesty, forthrightness, and straightforward thinking. This is the person people follow because they respect that person, and respect grows from trust as well. If your leader guides you correctly, then goals set forth by the client will have the greatest opportunity for success.

But, you have to know who is in charge. Therefore, when conflicts or questions arise, there is someone to make the needed decisions or point a person in the right direction to find answers.

The selection of an authoritative person should not come down to just a reward for a job well done, which is important and just, but it also has to do with the ability to manage conflict and varying personalities, and balance priorities. There is some truth in the Peter Principle, which states that people are promoted to their level of incompetence. Just so we understand, promoting people for good work is right, but with any promotion involving managing more people, the person should also possess the ability to resolve the conflicts between their staff or be given the opportunity to have the training that will give them the necessary skills to do so.

MANAGEMENT

Manufacturers must provide Guidance

Responsibility: The state of being responsible, accountable, or answerable; A duty, obligation, or liability for which someone is

> held accountable; The obligation to carry forward an assigned task to a successful conclusion.

So, even though you will have a team leader, as individual members of a team with conflicts, all must take responsibility. Each level of the staff depends on many different people working together. Each member is responsible for a functional area, and each must make use of their individual skill sets and experience in order to accomplish and produce effective and specific goals and objectives. It is the responsibility of each individual to make a concerted effort to ensure that the product is never affected in a negative fashion.

Every team will need an organizational flow of authority to provide guidance. All teams need to be able to address issues, concerns, and complaints by being provided resources and strategies for problem solving so that the mission of accurately resolving conflicts can succeed.

GOODWILL

> **Goodwill:** Goodwill is based on a company's reputation and relationships with customers, vendors and the community and its participation in trade-related activities. In broad terms, goodwill is a measure of how willing these individuals would be to continue doing business with a company.

People who give others a good impression of themselves will pass along that good impression and goodwill to the product they represent. The most successful Product Specialists are ambassadors of their product 24 hours a day. Somewhere between "24/7" and the time one steps on the product showroom floor, one needs to decide what their level of commitment is. When that is decided, one will discover their level of success.

AND FINALLY . . . .

It might be easy for some to say a Product Specialist simply specializes in a product. But, we believe the role of a PS involves far more than that. It is now your job to best represent, explain, celebrate, educate, and publicize your product so that it is readily understood and appreciated for the good it does.

Good Luck.

NOTES

NOTES

www.ingramcontent.com/pod-product-compliance
Lightning Source LLC
Chambersburg PA
CBHW060637280326
41933CB00012B/2072